Baby Joseph's

Heart

Big Physicists

Don't Cry

Chris Edge

Edge Family

Publishing

Baby Joseph's Heart

Baby Joseph's Heart

Big Physicists Don't Cry

Copyright © 2015 Edge Family Publishing

EdgeFamilyPublishing.com

ISBN: 0-9963379-2-X

ISBN-13: 978-0-9963379-2-2

Chris Edge

TABLE OF CONTENTS

Baby Joseph's Heart

Introduction

My wife, Karen, and I wrote brief descriptions of the births of our first two children, Lauren and David. Both children were miracle babies in the sense that there were very real dangers involved. Lauren's umbilical cord was around her neck during labor, and was difficult to extricate because it was shorter and thicker than normal. David's birth was without incident. However, as the umbilical cord was removed, our midwife realized to her amazement that it contained a large knot the size of a fist. The nurse commented that usually babies with such a knot are stillborn.

However, since the circumstances of Joseph's life were so extraordinary, and since so many friends and family were involved in praying for Joseph, we decided a somewhat more detailed recounting of events was in order. It is to all those who entered our lives with their prayers and tears (and to the One who answered them) that this story is dedicated.

Chris Edge

February 20, 2015

Chapter One

Crash and Burn

Joseph Dovaston Edge was born on Sunday, July 15, 1990, at 11:04 A.M. The labor was "normal" (if any labor can be said to be normal) in that the contractions began at 6:00 A.M., heavy labor began around 10:30 AM. Knowing that her hubby most likely would begin freaking out, Karen did not wake me during the first 45 minutes or so of her contractions. Instead, she attended to those last minute details like folding laundry.

When we arrived at the Family Birth Center at Children's Hospital in Saint Paul, MN, we became acquainted with our birthing nurse, Kathy Middlecamp. Kathy was a seasoned veteran who knew more about babies, birthing, and nursing than anyone I have ever known since. Her kindness, patience, and warmth filled the soul with a warm glow that radiates in our hearts 25 years later.

"Oh, I'll have the baby probably by 11:00." Karen said matter-of-factly to Kathy. I knew her statement had validity because of the pattern of the previous two births, but Kathy (I think) was amazed at how calm Karen was compared to most young moms about to deliver.

In the early stages, labor was uneventful. During the heavy pushing, there was a seven-minute period where the baby's heartbeat was in the 70's. However, that was remedied by finding the right position of Karen's body as labor continued. In short order, our little Joseph was born. The NICU team was on hand to check the baby out, but since everything seemed fine, Joseph was quickly placed in our arms. It was just past 11:00 A.M., as Karen had predicted! Nurse Kathy was even more amazed.

The first two days of Joseph's life couldn't have been more perfect. Karen and I had planned in advance for me to take charge of the kids and for her to recuperate at the hospital and bond with the baby. And bond they did. Joseph began nursing vigorously within the hour of his birth and continued to do so. Physically, Karen was recovering very quickly and kidded about not having to worry about post-partum depression. Everything was clicking perfectly together - or so it seemed.

Dr. Dennis O'Hare, one of our family doctors who had taken charge of checking Joseph after birth, wanted to perform a chest X-Ray just to confirm there were no abnormalities. He had heard a loud heart murmur, and wanted to check for a possible hole between the ventricles. The X-Ray came back showing the heart was on the large side of normal. Just to play it safe, Dennis requested an echocardiogram.

It was Tuesday afternoon. Karen had packed up her stuff and was ready to go home with our little guy. She had managed to quiet him down by nursing him just before the echocardiogram was performed. The procedure was taking a long time and I was trying to occupy the kids with Sesame Street while trying to control the knots that were growing in my stomach with each passing minute. As in all situations of facing unknown fears, I found myself praying that soon it would all be over, and my worries would be unfounded.

Another young nurse from the Family Birth Center came to where I was waiting with the kids. "The cardiologist wants to talk with you and your wife - go ahead, I'll watch the children." This was scary - doubly so because the nurse was long overdue to go home. Something big was clearly up.

When I entered the echocardiogram room, Karen was crying, holding Joseph close to her, and looking down at him. "The echo technician just kept looking and looking. She said, 'Well, as you can probably guess I've found something. I need to get the cardiologist here as soon as possible. Please wait.'" We waited together in fear and apprehension. Meanwhile, oblivious to the big to-do surrounding him, Joseph continued to sleep peacefully next to his mother's breast.

Dr. Stone soon arrived. "Now I want you to know that I had no idea that there even existed a person named Joseph Edge until just a few minutes ago. Let me just look at a few things here before we make any particular conclusions." He proceeded to study Joseph's heart on the monitor while the technician allowed him to view various positions and angles. "Have you already looked at the echocardiogram videos taken a few minutes ago?" I asked. Dr. Stone nodded, but made no answer as he studied intensely our little boy's heart on the monitor.

There were brief words of confirmation between himself and the echo technician. It didn't sound good.

Finally, Dr. Stone appeared satisfied with his observations. He escorted us back to the Family Birth Center, asking ominous but seemingly innocent questions to Karen like, "Now, you say you *do* have other children?" and "Now, how old are you again? Thirty-five? Oh, that's young."

He muttered something to the nurse about alerting the NICU and then proceeded to enlighten us about Joseph's condition. "Basically, little Joey's left ventricle hasn't developed. Oh, there's a little stub there, but for all intents and purposes, it doesn't exist. We call this condition a hypoplastic left ventricle. It doesn't happen terribly often, but often enough so that we are very familiar with it. Basically, these little babies appear fine at first, but as the cardio-vascular system makes the transition from being *in utero* to being on the outside where the lungs must obtain their own oxygen, they just - pardon the expression - crash and burn. Little Joey seems fine right this moment, but I want him under observation in the NICU in case he starts to go downhill."

He briefly touched on operations, including the heart transplant option. Very few hospitals had attempted heart transplants on infants at that time; one of the few was Loma Linda, California. However, this would require essentially relocating out there, with only a 50% chance of survival. The temporary option was the Norwood procedure, which would use the one working ventricle to pump blood to the body as well as to the lungs by creating a channel to the aorta.

That was it. We followed little Joseph back to the NICU (neonatal intensive care unit), were briefly introduced to Dr. Catherine Gotto who was in charge that evening, and saw our perfect baby becoming progressively attached to wires and tubes. We returned to our room, and alerted friends from our Catholic lay community, the Community of Christ the Redeemer (CCR). Karen was crying on the phone, "They think he's gonna die!"

****

Karen had always been transparent with her feelings.

I never had to guess what she was unhappy about. Good feelings or bad, joy or sorrow, irritated or excited, you knew exactly where she was at, and you knew exactly where you stood. This included tears when the situation called for it. This was one of the many attractive qualities I saw in her when we were dating. I had experienced people I loved who exploded with irritation or defensiveness. I had also experienced people who always had to be pried open like an oyster to find out what was bugging them.

Karen suffered from neither anger management nor cold shoulder tendencies, which meant small issues were always dealt with quickly before they became big. Spontaneity was always natural for her.

I suffered from multiple strikes against me when it came to expressing negative emotion. I was male, I came from British, academic stock, I was insecure, and worst of all I was a physicist. Emotions, especially negative feelings and spontaneous outbursts of grief, came with great difficulty. I am probably one of many who identified with the Vulcan portrayed by Leonard Nimoy, always feeling restrained when others felt free to cry their eyes out.

So even though the love I felt for little Joseph was beyond words, and even though my heart felt sick at the sudden discovery that we might lose this beautiful precious baby boy, there were no tears. There was only shock and fervent prayer for a solution to this fatal heart defect.

****

Within half an hour after Karen's phone call, friends were trickling into the room. By the end of the hour, the room was full of our adopted St. Paul family.

Karen and I were from the east coast, and had no family in the area. When 3M offered the job to work in research and development in Minnesota, we were a little bit skeptical to say the least. We had friends out east who were from Minnesota. We had also listened to "A Prairie Home Companion" quite a bit. So we had a pretty good idea of the intensity of the winters in this state. Traveling halfway across the country to a Siberian climate with no friends or relatives seemed a bit risky.

However, when I came out for my job interview in 1985, I got together with an acquaintance from Virginia who had moved here with his wife. Paul raved about the Twin Cities, about the culture, the people, the relaxed family orientation of the region. He also raved about the Catholic lay community he had discovered. He related stories about individuals whose boilers died in the middle of winter, and about how members of the community chipped in to get them a new boiler because they didn't have the money.

That type of communal commitment was exactly what I was looking for, so based on that and other similar stories, we decided to accept the position and move to Minnesota, Land of a Thousand Lakes.

Even before this urgent situation, the Community of Christ the Redeemer (or "the Community" as we generally referred to it) had already become like family with our first two kids, giving us used baby clothing, diapers, and all the usual odds and ends one needs when starting a family.

And so, they were there for us now in our room at Children's Hospital - crying with us, praying with us, talking with us in our utter disbelief. Over and over again Karen and I felt that this had to be a dream, and soon one of us would wake up and it would be Tuesday morning again. But we didn't wake up, and we knew that our perfect baby had a fatal heart defect.

There were many hugs and tears that evening - and much hope. As we gradually began to pray together as a group, the head coordinator of the Community, Jim Kolar, requested that we all be silent for a while, listen in our hearts for our Lord to speak, and receive guidance about how to pray. Several people shared a similar theme that each had received, and that Jim summed up: "I have not brought forth life from the womb simply to die. My intent is Life." The prayer that kept coming to my lips was, "Lord, I am not worthy to receive You, but say the word and my son shall be healed."

Later that night we met the other cardiologist, Dr. Sutton. He had received further news from the University, that upon evaluating the echo videos, they concluded that Joseph also had a seriously defective valve between the right atrium and the right ventricle (a strike against him) as well as a transposed aorta, meaning that the aorta was on the right ventricle along with the pulmonary artery (a strike in his favor). In a sense, part of the Norwood procedure had already been accomplished. "He's just got a two-chamber heart, like a turtle," said Dr. Mike Mallinger, our good friend and family dentist.

Mike was quickly enlisted, along with our friend Laurie Wrobel, to be the godparents for Joseph. Our deacon, Tom Langlois, had arrived, and was ready to perform Joseph's baptism. By now Dr. Sutton had recommended, and Dr. O'Hare agreed, to implement a full life support system including ventilator and IV heart medications Dopamine and Dobutamine to make the heart beat vigorously, plus Prostaglandins which would keep the ductus open, the vessel which helped channel blood to the aorta.

The ductus we came to learn is part of the temporary circulatory system that allows oxygen from the mother through the umbilical cord to be pumped by the baby's heart. Once the baby is born, these connections are no longer needed as blood proceeds to get oxygen from the lungs. Hence, they naturally close. With Joseph's lack of left ventricle, his open ductus was helping to keep him alive.

We proceeded back to the NICU. The nurses were saints in their compassion for us and in their tenderness for Joseph. The Children's Hospital had a policy of encouraging parents to hold their babies even though they were hooked up to ventilators and IV's. It was scary for us to hold Joseph with so many lines attached - I was always afraid of snagging or breaking one of the precious lifelines to his body. Karen held our son while Tom proceeded to welcome him into the Body of Christ through the waters of baptism. He laid a miniature stole over him like a priest might wear as a substitute for a baptismal gown, which we had had no time to procure. Somehow, the centuries-old Christian symbols on the stole seemed incongruous against the sterile sophisticated technology of tubes and wires that had quite enveloped our little Joseph.

By now, it was getting late. Before leaving, friends asked for specific prayer requests to share with the larger group. The two requests we made were 1) for Joseph to be healed either directly or through surgery and 2) for guidance and wisdom about how to proceed. It was clear that a choice would soon have to be made. An operation similar to the Norwood procedure had perhaps a 30% chance of survival, with a second major surgery being required in a few months. Then hopefully the child would live long enough to do a transplant, perhaps at age two. Alternatively, we could unhook Joseph, and hold him for the few remaining hours or perhaps day or two before he died. Both choices seemed grim, and we had no clear indication from the medical community about which route was best.

We asked Dr. O'Hare what he would do for his own child if he were in this situation. We felt comfortable asking him since we knew him well and he knew us well through our mutual church involvement. Dennis carefully responded that he would rather think and pray for a day or two before answering. The fact that we knew he would give us a very well thought-out answer was a comfort, since we really had no idea what to do.

That night we slept snuggled together in our Family Birth Center room. To say that we were emotionally exhausted would be an understatement. Perhaps because we were so tired, we slept well. When the morning came, we both awoke with that same feeling of wishing the whole previous day had been a dream and that Joseph was sleeping in his bassinet in our room. Reality sank in again when we returned to the NICU and began our early morning vigil of taking turns holding our precious baby.

Chapter Two

Letting Go

Dr. O'Hare (Dennis to us) came during his usual early morning rounds (he said that his tombstone would read "Chronic Sleep Deprivation"). He quietly knelt by us as Karen wept and we talked and held Joseph. Finally, as our family physician, he ordered us to go out and get some breakfast. He stressed the importance of taking care of ourselves because of the potentially long road ahead. Furthermore, our two other beautiful children would need two strong healthy parents during the rough days to come.

Dr. Sutton came by to confirm that the tricuspid valve between the right atrium and ventricle was failing severely, and that the infant heart surgeon at the hospital felt that open-heart surgery to fix a valve on such a small baby would be out of the question. It still was not clear whether there were three, two, or only one reasonable option.

We did go out to eat, and combined it with returning to our house to pack for further days at the hospital. It was hard to keep from crying as we looked at the menu and wondered whether we had the heart to order anything, but once we began to eat our appetites returned. Karen hadn't eaten for over 24 hours, which is pretty bad when you consider that after giving birth, her body must have needed lots of nutrition to help recover. But with all that had been going on, food just hadn't been on either of our radar screens.

The rest of Wednesday was devoted to being in the NICU with Joseph. Many friends from our church community came by, as well as friends from 3M. The memory of them is a like a blur of tears. I remember especially Jim Kolar visiting and once again praying for the Lord to work in a powerful way. Later, Fr. Joe Menker came by, the unofficial chaplain of the CCR, and performed the sacrament of the Anointing of the Sick. In the early evening, Deacon Tom Langlois came with a fellow Deacon from the Indian reservation in South Dakota. He apparently had a very successful ministry of healing the sick there, including his own son who had completely recovered from bone cancer a couple of years earlier. Tom's friend shared a vision that he had of the skies opening and of Mary holding Joseph snugly in her arms. That vision became imprinted in my heart during the days ahead whenever Joseph was hooked up to life support.

That evening, upstairs in the chapel of Children's Hospital, there were 50 or 60 people from our church community praying for Joseph and for us. People were spilling out into the halls. From all accounts, it was a time of incredibly deep prayer, and many said that God was present to them more powerfully than they had ever felt before. As things wound down, various people came down for a quick farewell just to see how we were holding up, and to give us a hug.

So ended the second day of crisis. We slept in a small closet-like room near the NICU and wondered what would happen tomorrow.

Thursday morning arrived. We returned to our post in the NICU and waited for Dr. O'Hare to arrive. He came to us and gently pulled up a stool. "I've thought carefully about this, and I'm ready to tell you what I would do for my own child." We listened eagerly through our tears for what he would say. "Firstly, you've got to remember your primary responsibility as parents and that is to get your child to heaven. You've already done that. You've loved Joseph and had him baptized. There is no question about where he will be if he dies. Secondly, God can heal Joseph's heart if He wants to. He can even allow his heart to function and keep him alive just as it is. He can perform surgery far better than we can.

"Since Joseph's valve is so bad, I'd say his odds of surviving the Norwood procedure are minimal. I think the choice is whether to let Joseph die in your arms or on the operating table."

By this time, our other friend and family doctor had arrived, Dr. Ron Otremba. Together, they comforted us and held us while we wept in agreement with Dennis' conclusion. Through her tears, Karen said, "Before Joseph was born I was ready to switch clinics because of the long drive. Now after all this there's no way I'd ever switch. I don't care if I have to drive to Wisconsin and wait all day to be seen!"

Our doctor friends left us. Finally, Dr. Stone arrived. Karen and I tried to get right to the point and tell him our decision. However, it appeared that Dr. Stone was afraid that we had decided to intervene surgically; he insisted on starting from the beginning. For the next 45 minutes he reiterated the status of Joseph's heart, all the surgical options, and one by one explained their pitfalls.

When he was done, he spoke heavily and said, "Now, I can present all these facts to you, but as your cardiologist I feel that I would be doing you a disservice if I simply left you with all this information without any conclusion of what I think this all means. Based on the severity of his condition - and I know this isn't easy - my recommendation is to just let him go. I *don't* recommend we operate."

He waited to see our reaction. We proceeded to explain that we were in full agreement with his conclusions. "You guys have done a great job and have done all you can do. Since Joseph's condition appears to be medically hopeless, we feel that the time had come to redirect our focus. Human technology has met its limit. Now we'll focus on the supernatural rather than the natural. We will be praying that God heals Joseph. That is our request. If Joseph is healed, we will be overjoyed, and you guys can all come to his six-month birthday! If he dies, that will be OK, too, because we know where he will be."

I think Dr. Stone was a bit stunned by this response. Apparently this was not the typical reaction he received from parents faced with similar circumstances. It was as though we had just lifted a 10-ton boulder off his shoulders! "That is such a great response! I wish I had a tape recorder to capture that!" He looked so relieved. Later, nurses told us horror stories of parents clinging to life with their infants, demanding extraordinary measures that resulted only in a long slow painful death for the child who had to be attended to by the doctors and nurses who could only watch helplessly. Right or wrong, it is always the parents' choice to make.

We thanked Dr. Stone for all his help, and began talking about the details of where to go from here. It was arranged that we could have one of the Family Birth Center rooms as a hospice where we could have privacy until Joseph died, yet have the nursing staff available to help us through the difficult transition of death. As we left the hospital to make arrangements to have the Lauren and David brought over, I said to Dr. Stone, "By the way, if Joseph lives, we'll expect you to sign the papers that this is a *bona fide* miracle!" He assured us that he would be delighted. As we continued to talk with doctors and nurses, it became clear that the medical community agreed with the decision 100%. We could not have received a clearer answer to our prayer for guidance.

Mike and Christi had kept Lauren and David overnight the first night of the crisis. The next day they stayed with our neighbors, Andy and Dorie, who brought them to the hospital. We offered for them to stay with us when the time came to unhook Joseph. Even though it was hard for them, they agreed. Meanwhile, our church community had gone into Red Alert, and quite a gathering was preparing to assemble in the hospital chapel to pray for a miracle when Joseph was unhooked.

We prepared the children for what might happen, and were ready to receive our son into our arms for the last time. We were very direct and open with Lauren (4), and with David (2) to the degree they could understand. David was a pretty typical two-year-old boy so he knew something was wrong with Joseph, but didn't fully understand what was the matter. Lauren, being two years older and the first-born, had a fairly mature understanding of the world around her. She understood about Joseph's heart being sick, and that he might die. She also knew of our hope, and prayed with us for Joseph to get better.

The hospital was well staffed for all situations, including the death of an infant. This included a child psychologist to help young siblings prepare for a baby's death. The psychologist spent several minutes with Lauren trying to help her understand the upcoming event that was about to occur. Lauren was a bit confused with what the counselor was trying to accomplish, and concluded that she perhaps didn't understand the medical situation. Lauren proceeded to explain Joseph's heart, and what was wrong with it, using her little fist as a visual aid. She seemed fully aware of what was about to happen, and seemed ready to face it because of her certainty that Joseph would be in heaven.

Meanwhile, our church community was ready for prayer in the chapel, with the usual vibrant singing and people spilling out into the halls. What amazed me was how considerate and organized they were. One person was always responsible to monitor who came down to visit us so that our needs would be met without overwhelming us. Just knowing of their presence was a source of strength and courage for us.

We went to the NICU and waited while the nurse proceeded to disconnect the tubes. "How long do you think he'll last?" Karen asked. "Oh, I think he'll last at least an hour," said the nurse, apparently thinking that this would sound good to parents expecting a few minutes. Karen, however, was not thinking in terms of minutes, and her heart sank. Soon, our son was free from the technological web that had surrounded him. Karen took him in her arms, and we slowly walked back to the Family Birth Center.

I had sent word about Joseph's condition to our local Catholic parish, the Nativity of our Lord, and suspected that Father Pat Lannon would appear. Sure enough, his timing was incredible! He appeared just as all this was going on, and joined our procession back to our room. Being open and warm-hearted, Fr. Pat sat himself down in a rocker and held out his arms. "Come on, let me hold him!" At this point, Karen was loath to release Joseph, not knowing how long he would last, but Fr. Pat obviously wanted to hold him, so with great effort she gently handed him over.

Fr. Pat held him long enough to give Joseph a "Coochy-coo!" I then suggested that he join our Community upstairs for a while in prayer, which he promptly did. In retrospect, we both realized how symbolic Fr. Pat had been at that moment, because it was as though Christ Himself had sat there in the rocker asking us to let go of Joseph and to trust Him with our precious little guy.

Years later, Father Pat recounted what happened after he left us. He headed up to the chapel with a long-time friend of his and nurse at Children's hospital. Apparently, she had never experienced a charismatic community before. As they entered the chapel, she muttered to Fr. Pat, *"What are they all doing?"* He muttered back to her from the side of his mouth, *"They're speaking in tongues."* She quietly asked further, *"Well what are they saying?"* *"I have no idea,"* Fr.

Pat responded. *"I don't have the gift of interpretation of tongues."*

Meanwhile, back in our hospice room, we all took turns holding Joseph and loving him. We especially wanted Lauren and David to hold their brother. We wanted them to know that they had been a good sister and brother to him, and that in no way were they responsible for what was going to happen.

Andy and Dorie stayed until it was time for Lauren and David to go home and go to bed. Mike and Christi stayed with us. They had been in the few photos that were taken earlier during the baptism. Together we reflected gratefully on the miracle of having received such clear guidance. Now we hoped beyond hope for the other miracle – the miracle of healing, which would have been far beyond any possible medical solution.

It got late, and our friends left, as did our army of intercessors in the chapel. Our nurse Cheryl had started the 11:00 P.M. shift, and was going to spend the night near us, to monitor Joseph's heart and breathing. In this way she could prepare us and guide us down the frightening path that neither of us felt prepared to face.

Chapter Three

Turtle Heart

By now a few hours had passed, and the nurses were sensing intuitively based on experience that Joseph would last until morning. Cheryl gave us an update every hour. Initially, Joseph had a pretty normal heart rate and breathing. "His breathing is about 50 per minute, heartbeat 150." Little Joseph had been awake quite a bit since being unhooked. He tried to cry, but his voice was pathetically hoarse from the ventilator he had been on.

We acted on the assumption that by some miracle, Joseph might live, so we dribbled water and milk into his mouth from the preemie bottles a little at a time whenever he was willing. We now saw the physical manifestation of his condition. Each time he began to suck, his tiny feet turned purple, nearly black. It required a strong stomach to feed him and back off when his heart seemed to strain itself.

That night, we slept on and off together with Joseph in the bed, Karen on one side, I on the other. Cheryl said it was quite a picture, this little dying baby surrounded by a living circle of flesh. Several times I nearly fell off the bed until Cheryl raised the side railing on my side! Both Karen and I felt a great peace, regardless of what was to happen, now that our little boy was in our arms, and God was in His heaven.

The night of half-sleep brought slow changes. "His respiration is 60." Later, "It's up to 70." By morning, it was up to about 80. But Joseph was still alive, and *very* alert! By now, I was convinced God was doing something. Karen shared my hope, but feared to rejoice too hastily. After all, the doctor did say Joseph could last a couple of days. Dr. Dennis O'Hare came to visit. He appreciated my enthusiasm, but like Karen felt that there was little doubt that he was dying, and didn't want me to torture myself with miracles that had not yet occurred. He did, however, fully encourage us to keep praying, because it clearly was not over yet.

After Dennis left, I felt sad that my optimism was clearly premature. A young girl in our Community, Elaine, had left a nice note of support along with a bottle of water from Lourdes. I remembered a suggestion from one of the guys not just to anoint Joseph, but actually to allow him to drink some of the waters from this faraway place of miracles. On a compulsion, I opened his preemie bottle and poured in a significant quantity of the water into his milk. Joseph chugged it down!

At about that same time, we began noticing that Joseph's feet looked better when he ate. In fact, the whole day went well. Somehow, having survived the night, we both felt very prepared for life or death. There was something about death during the night that seemed fearful. But in daylight, even death seemed more natural and less to be feared. Joseph looked pretty darn good for a dying baby!

The day went quickly with lots of time sharing with the nurses, especially with Kathy, who had been our labor nurse. Now she was with us again and quietly went through in detail what the dying process would be like for Joseph when it happened. She stressed the peacefulness and the naturalness of it. It was so good to have her and other empathetic folks around. Our daytime nurse from the NICU, Peggy Noel, was our quiet, easygoing companion. She was happy for us that Joseph had lasted so long, as opposed to dying within minutes. She gently pointed out however that the symptoms of severe heart failure were still there, and that we should not mistake his reasonably good appearance for health.

That night, we again prepared for death while praying for life. Slowly, Joseph's respiration began rising, which indicated that his heart was failing more and more, and that fluid was building up in his lungs. We nestled down together, with Joseph again in the middle of this human doughnut we had formed around him. We finally fell asleep, including Joseph, while Cheryl and the Lord watched over us. His respiration now was 100 breaths per minute, twice the normal rate.

Around 4:00 A.M., we awoke to the sound of Joseph crying with a piercing scream. He had apparently regained his voice after the hoarseness from the ventilator! My immediate response was "He's dying! He's in pain! Where's the morphine?!" But Karen and Cheryl were both hearing Joseph differently.

"Just cool it for a second!" Karen said while Cheryl got the bottle. Our little guy, it turned out, was quite hungry, and quickly drained the bottle. Soon, the morning light arrived, and our Joseph was really quite lively, and now vocal to boot. As I showered that morning, I recalled reading a book, *Heartsounds*, that was the real life account of a doctor who had suffered a heart attack. I remembered that the key medication to give to a chronic heart failure patient was a diuretic, which drains the fluid from the lungs. Otherwise, heart failure patients died very prematurely from drowning in their own fluid. As I showered I felt a burning conviction, as though the Lord Himself was saying, "You *must* get him diuretics *soon*!" I talked to Peggy about it and she agreed, "*I* would do it."

When Dennis arrived, I pulled him to the side and shared my strong sense. He did not discount the feeling. Instead he checked Joseph out. As he heard the solid heart beat and saw Joseph scream bloody murder, he smiled thoughtfully and said he would talk immediately with the NICU doctors. He soon returned and said they agreed that a diuretic was not an extraordinary measure. Once they began the treatment, I felt a great sense of relief.

By Sunday morning, Joseph's breathing had returned to the 70's, where it remained during the weeks ahead. Peggy said, "We're going to give this guy a bath!" and that she did. Dr. Stone arrived, and we began pressing him about:

1) Why was our dying baby still alive?

2) Why had he actually *improved*, both in appetite and in the color of his extremities?

Dr. Stone conjectured at first that the vessels of the lungs had opened up, permitting more flow of blood. "But," I said, "wouldn't that mean that there was less blood going to the rest of the body since he's only got one chamber?" Well, yes, one would think so he seemed to think. Right after that, Peggy weighed Joseph and checked his blood pressure. It was no different from when he had been on life support.

For the first time since Joseph's crisis began, we had something concrete to point to that suggested some form of divine healing. We felt comfortable leaving Joseph in Peggy's able care, and went for a stroll to the Denny's Restaurant near the hospital. I will never forget that morning, because it was a beautiful cool summer day, and the St. Paul Cathedral was ringing the bells for Sunday Mass. It seemed as though all heaven was rejoicing for Joseph and for us. When we came back, Peggy shared that when she took Joseph to the NICU for his weighing, he was screaming like a banshee. The other nurses gathered around saying, "That's not Joseph Edge! That's not a dying baby!" She just smiled.

The following day, Dr. Sutton came to see us. We posed the same question to him that we had posed to Dr. Stone. This time, the conclusion made a great deal of sense. "I think his valve is starting to work - that would allow his whole heart to function much better." We shared his speculations with friends involved in medicine and they were much amazed. Typically valves don't heal or improve. They get worse, rather like torn cartilage. Later, Dr. Sutton confirmed with the echocardiogram that it seemed to him that the valve was working much better.

That night, a number of people from our church community came to the chapel to pray. There was much hope and much thanksgiving for the events that had taken place. The night before, Mike and Christi, and Tom and

Laurie came by with Champagne to celebrate Joseph's first week of life. Friends helped in so many ways. One 3M friend, Dr. John Souter, made a trip to the airport with his frequent flier coupon to acquire a ticket for Karen's sister, Carol. As a result, she was able to fly from Rochester N.Y. the next day and became our "nanny" for Lauren and David. We never forgot that generous, spontaneous gesture of support from John and from Carol, too.

The night she arrived, we took a break with her and went to a downtown restaurant called the "Heartthrob Café" that touted servers on roller-skates. To this day Karen remembers that on the menu one of the items read "I want my baby back ribs!"

By Tuesday, the medical community had taken an about face. "Take this kid home! It's a sin to have a healthy child like this in the hospital!" Karen and I were overwhelmed and confused. One minute, Joseph was about to die. Now, he still was missing his left ventricle, but he looked great, aside from a bit of jaundice, and had a healthy appetite. At first the doctors said take him home on the weekend. Then they said take him home tomorrow. Before we knew it, the NICU was advocating taking him home this very day! Before we knew it, arrangements were made to connect us with home health care, papers were signed, and our hungry, alert little heart patient was no longer a patient of the hospital. We took him home.

The next three days were amazingly normal. Karen and I stayed up around the clock feeding Joseph, because he still was only strong enough to eat about one ounce of milk during a feeding. Aside from that, Joseph was a beautiful normal baby. We had him in our arms most of the time, which was feasible since Carol was there to help. By now, church community families took turns bringing us wonderful meals every night.

By Friday, Joseph looked more yellow with jaundice. The bilirubin test showed that he was up at the high end of normal. Dr. Ron was uncomfortable with that, so on Friday night, we returned to the hospital to have Joseph put under lights. We arrived just before the end of the evening shift. Joseph looked so good that the doctors put him in a non-critical status. We explained to the nurses that Joseph needed to use the preemie bottles and nipples. After they got him situated under the lights, we went home and got some much needed sleep.

In the morning, everything sounded OK at the hospital, so we took time to play with Lauren and David before heading in. When we arrived, we noticed that people were worried. It turned out that Joseph had not eaten well during the night and morning, and was dehydrated. Unfortunately, a miscommunication had occurred. The message that Joseph could only drink from preemie bottles had not been passed on. His lack of eating was attributed to the jaundice. He needed IV fluids to counter the dehydration.

Due to his weak heart, Joseph's veins were very difficult to get IV's into. The neo-natal surgeon was called, and he proceeded to do a "cut down". This meant cutting open Joseph's ankle to get the IV in. It took about 45 minutes even with the surgeon's skill to finally get the line in. Joseph cried, but after it was over, he seemed fine, and the nurse let us hold him for a while. They gave us a preemie bottle filled with Karen's milk, and within minutes, Joseph had consumed it. He still appeared hungry, so another bottle was prepared, and he consumed that as well.

Satisfied that Joseph still had a good appetite, we burped him for quite a while to make sure he wouldn't vomit his big meal. Finally, the nurse said that Joseph should go back under the lights, and that before he did, a chest X-Ray should be made. Joseph looked very comfortable, so we gave him back to the nurse and went downstairs for some lunch. We felt good that our little guy had eaten well, and figured we'd have him home pretty soon.

Chapter Four

The Roller Coaster

When we got back, Joseph was under the lights on his tummy, blindfold on. With horror, we realized that he was heaving up and down, almost like a fish out of water. The nurse assumed that he was just gasping for breath because he had been crying hard for the last half hour.

Perhaps because he had been doing so well, the nurse didn't realize the severity of his condition - we never felt comfortable letting Joseph cry for more than a few minutes. The nurse took Joseph out, and to our even greater horror we realized that his eyes were open with a dead stare straight out into space. He was gasping and crying weakly. Then Joseph's new nurse, who had just started her shift, immediately realized the seriousness of Joseph's state, and ran to get the cardiologist. He confirmed that Joseph had almost no pulse. "Do you want us to do something, or do you want to hold him while he dies?" they asked. "*Do something, of course!*" we responded. They proceeded to put Joseph under a small oxygen tent and placed an oxygen saturation sensor on his hand.

By now, Tom and Laurie had arrived. Karen couldn't bear to watch Joseph in this state, so Tom and Laurie waited outside in the hallway with Karen, crying with her, holding her, and praying with her. Meanwhile, back in the NICU,

Joseph was fighting for life. His oxygen saturation (or "sats" for short) was at about 50% - normal would be over 90%. This was not good considering he had nearly pure oxygen surrounding his head.

Knowing that I probably looked a bit odd (if not fanatical), I knelt next to Joseph's incubator and held his tiny hand. Using his fingers for beads, I prayed the rosary with all my heart and soul, glancing at his sats level for signs of hope every few minutes.

"Hail Mary, full of grace..."

Periodically, I went out and updated Karen and our friends, then continued to kneel and pray using Joseph's fingers as tiny beads of flesh.

"Hail Mary, full of grace..."

"He doesn't look **too** bad, does he?" I said hopefully to Joseph's nurse after a while. "His color looks **very** bad, " she countered.

"Hail Mary, full of grace..."

The head of the unit instructed the nurse to administer some Prostaglandins to open up Joseph's ductus, which as I mentioned before, is the vessel between the aorta and pulmonary arteries. Perhaps that would help – it obviously couldn't hurt under the circumstances.

"Hail Mary, full of grace..."

About that time, Joseph's levels began rising. Slowly, but surely, his sats increased. About an hour after nearly dying,

Joseph's levels were back to normal. There was no question in either of our minds that our Lord, His Mother, and the good doctor had brought our son back to us, at least for now.

That night, there was intensive prayer at the chapel. Many of our friends from the church community were there. We had never wept so fiercely before in our lives, nor prayed with more agony in our hearts. Yet, through it all there was a bittersweet mixture of love with the sorrow, the love we had for our little Joseph, the love of such beautiful friends who "weep with those who weep and rejoice with those who rejoice", and the love and hope we had towards God who was clearly present in the midst of a hopeless and horrifying situation.

Finally, the doctors arrived, having performed another echocardiogram. Josephs' heart looked bad. The valve was now malfunctioning severely, which made Joseph's prospects quite grim. The recommendation was to put him on complete life support until Monday, when a heart catheter would reveal the intricacies of Joseph's heart, and indicate whether there was some unforeseen hope. The head of the NICU, Dr. Boros, was a very laid back, very wise older doctor, "When I read Joseph's file, I could tell that Joseph is the kind of patient that makes medical people **very** uncomfortable. He just doesn't fit into any category. He breaks all the medical rules. When you expect him to die, he goes on living like nothing's wrong. When you think he's stable, suddenly he almost dies. Joseph is simply Joseph!"

Sunday morning arrived with scary news. We had spent the night at home, figuring that since Joseph had now been given a critical status and was on life support, there was little risk of oversight. That morning, the nurse suggested we come in quickly, because blood had been found in Joseph's stool. "He's had a hemorrhage," we thought as we drove to the hospital. As we entered the hospital, the bells of the Cathedral were ringing. This time, it was as though heaven were ringing its bells to welcome Joseph home.

Joseph, however, had other plans. The blood, it turned out, was a normal result of putting the ventilator into his windpipe, and was of no consequence. The head of the unit was very comfortable with Joseph's current stability. The poor nurse felt very guilty for scaring us, but we told her we'd rather be happy with premature bad news than disappointed with premature good news.

The next day, Joseph was again stable. His jaundice was now quite under control, which Dr. Boros had predicted. Our special nurse Peggy was on duty again that morning, and was to assist Dr. Sutton in the heart catheter procedure. Karen and I waited in the comfortable nursing rooms while Joseph was wheeled to the catheter lab. Our friend Dorie from across the street arrived; Dr. Ron and Dr. Dennis dropped by. Soon, Randy Mueller, one of the full time coordinators of our community, came and waited with us. Every now and then, Peggy would come and give us an update. It took hours. They tried to get the catheter first in one leg, then the other. Randy sat patiently with us, mainly listening and being a true friend and support. Now and then, one of us would share a thought, a prayer, or Randy would share a quote from a book he had brought.

Finally, the catheterization was done. Dr. Sutton came by and said everything had gone well, with no complications from the procedure. He came back a little later, sat down and explained what he and Dr. Stone had seen. The valve was malfunctioning moderately to severely. Furthermore, the separation between the right and left upper chambers was not open as was originally thought, but rather was very constricted, and probably was closing. When that happened, there would be no more oxygenated blood returning from the lungs, and death would be immediate.

He wanted to meet the next day with other cardiologists in the area to discuss the results of the heart catheter. Till then, Joseph would be kept on life support. We spent most of the day taking turns sitting next to him. We didn't want to disturb him too much - we felt better letting the sedatives keep him drowsy so he wouldn't be too uncomfortable with all the tubes.

The next day, Tuesday, Dr. Dennis met with us in the morning after the meeting of the cardiologists that he had attended. "It really sounds like there's nothing that can be done. Not only does he have the bad valve, the closing separation between the upper chambers, but Joseph also has a stenosis at the base of the aorta." What this meant was that the aorta was almost completely blocked. As Dr. Sutton later explained, the aorta was so blocked that they could not get the catheter into the aorta. Much of Joseph's circulation was probably coming from the vessels to the lungs via the small ductus between them and the aorta.

Whereas the previous week we had hoped that Joseph was better than originally thought because he was doing so well, it now appeared that he was far, far worse than originally thought, if that were possible. It was clear that everyone was in agreement that Joseph's case really was hopeless, and that we should unhook him again, and love him till the end came. "You guys have been on a roller coaster!" Dr. Sutton said, and his words were echoed by a lot of friends.

For the second time, we prepared the children and made arrangements to have a room to keep Joseph. Lauren and David arrived, eager to see their little brother again. The nurse began weaning Joseph gradually from the respirator. Before long, he was breathing fine on his own.

We brought him back to the room and passed him around. Randy was there for us again, and shared our joy at having our Joseph back where he belonged. Over the next couple of days, we wandered around the hospital, but always gravitated back to the Family Birth Center. Technically, the Family Birth Center is only for patients who are about to have or have just had a baby. However, our various nurse friends were very welcoming, which was nice because we greatly preferred the homey atmosphere.

It was so good not to have Joseph all hooked up. No matter how bad his prognosis, we always felt better once he was in our arms. Over the two days, Joseph remained stable, once again defying the laws of medical science. His appetite was good, which he needed because his poor frail body had now lost nearly a pound since birth. While he was on life support, only glucose was given, for fear that nutrients would clog the only good line into his body. Now Joseph's legs had become little twigs and his buttocks were non-existent. But he seemed comfortable, and drank his milk as long as it was no more than an ounce at a time.

We had visits from several special friends during this peaceful time of waiting. In particular, Bill and Carolyn Dower came to hang out with us and with Joseph. The Dowers had been our first welcoming contacts here in the Twin Cities. Bill and I worked in the same lab at 3M, and together we had seen our families begin to grow. They too were like second family for Lauren and David to stay with during this crisis.

After the two days, we felt comfortable taking Joseph home. Our attitude now was that Joseph's heart was obviously not healed, but that somehow God had hooked him up to a divine life support system. There was comfort in that, somehow, because if Joseph were to die, it would be the Lord beckoning him to come home. Then again, maybe Joseph would simply go on living.

Karen's sister Carol had taken good care of the kids during this second round of crises. Whereas before, there was some fear of becoming close to a dying baby, now Joseph looked so "good" that she was quite comfortable holding him. And he was so damn cute! The only freaky thing at first was that his eyes veered consistently off to the left. Whereas before, there had been significant eye contact, now there was none. "Dear Lord," we prayed, "Please bring him back to us before he dies!"

Like many others, this prayer was answered in due time. Carol and Karen first noticed that Joseph really liked staring at the picture of the Cat in the Hat. Gradually, his big eyes would begin to look back at us when we held him and fed him through the days and nights. One by one, families from our neighborhood and our community came by to see little Joseph. Lauren and David were proud of how they could hold him and feed him from his little preemie bottle. We were careful, though, about hand washing and not letting anyone with a cold near him. We had been warned that an infection could be deadly in his condition.

The next three and a half weeks don't need a lot of description, because they were so normal. They were not dramatically different from any other family that has taken a newborn home. The only difference was that Joseph desperately needed nutrition. The only way to do that was to feed him as much as possible every two hours around the clock. Because of his weakness, feeding him was a laborious task, taking half an hour to an hour.

On top of the challenge of feeding him in his weakened state, Joseph would easily lose the nutrition we had so carefully fed him by throwing it all back up again. This included medications. As a result, we did the best we could by tracking all his food intake, medication intake, and losses of all the above due to vomiting in order to confirm he was receiving enough nutrition and medication each day.

Joseph's primary source of milk was from Karen. Since he was too weak to nurse after his heart defect began affecting him, Karen was initially using a manual breast pump to extract milk for him. As this became progressively more difficult, the hospital arranged for us to have an electric breast pump. In addition, nursing moms from the CCR donated their milk as well to make sure we had enough.

Joseph would have severe gastric pain after he had sucked the first fraction of an ounce of milk. We found that the preemie bottles no longer worked, because his suck was too strong, collapsing the nipple. Yet, normal bottles and nipples were hard to suck on in his weak state. Somehow, with much effort, Joseph would take his milk slowly around the clock. As we continued to monitor his intake, we found that he was just above the minimum for survival fairly consistently each day.

Even with Carol there to help us, our hands were very full. By now, I had begun working at home. My boss at 3M, Ran Bedekar, was wonderfully supportive, as were my fellow employees. In fact, Carol Ferguson, whose husband Ian managed our huge project, had Lauren and David at their house several times. The kids would grow impatient to visit the "Fergons".

As the weeks went by, Joseph matured and developed, at least in terms of his personality. By the end of the second week home, he began to smile and laugh. When our neighbors and close friends, Bonnie and Neal, had his grandmother at their house, we spent time together. It was the grandmother's perceptive eye that noticed Joseph's first smile. "That baby is living on love," she asserted.

To our eyes, it seemed that Joseph had put on weight. His thighs and buttocks now had at least some fat on them. But his weight was merely redistributed. After two and a half weeks, we took Joseph for a check-up with Dr. Dennis at the clinic. Karen was very encouraged by the fact that he was still alive and appeared stable. Dennis gently tempered her enthusiasm. "You know, Karen, a healthy baby would have gained 5 – 7 ounces per week after birth.

41

Joseph is not yet back at his birth weight. He's clearly not thriving." Dennis confirmed that eventually, he would die of malnutrition if not from a direct heart failure. This was clearly the truth, but I remember there were a lot of tears as we begrudgingly agreed that despite looking relatively normal, our baby was dying.

Chapter Five

Transplant

Joseph's primary NICU nurse, Peggy, kept in close touch as did our midwives and Family Birth Center friends. Kathy Middlecamp was really helpful with feeding techniques. With help from a syringe, and tips from Kathy, we even got Joseph to re-learn how to nurse. Quite a miracle that was, after five weeks. Somehow, nothing seemed to increase the quantity of Joseph's intake.

Finally, Peggy said one day, "Did you hear they performed an infant heart transplant at the U of M?" I didn't think too much about her comment at first, because I assumed it was a fluke, a desperate attempt at life requested by demanding parents. But soon after, a neighbor interning at the NICU also made subtle hints. Since Joseph was still alive we might want to ask our doctors about taking a new approach, like considering a transplant. The fact that Joseph was doing as well as he was for a baby with his condition seemed to indicate that the valve had once again improved.

Finally, I called Dr. Dennis and then our cardiologist Dr. Sutton. Both were supportive of calling the head of the University transplant team, Dr. Liz Braunlin. Dr. Braunlin was very encouraging regarding the quality of life of children who have received a heart transplant. Somehow, I had the impression transplant kids were a bit like AIDS patients. Liz assured me however that they could attend school normally, do sports, and fight off infections reasonably well. And yes, they had indeed performed their first infant heart transplant. They also had experience with small children heart transplants, fifteen in all.

That Sunday, six weeks after Joseph's birth, the Community of Christ the Redeemer had an outdoor Mass and picnic at Hidden Falls Park. It was a gorgeous sunny day. After the service, Randy asked that Karen and I share about this new transplant possibility with our Community. For several minutes, everyone prayed quietly for Joseph with outstretched hands. After a bit of squirming, even Lauren and David proceeded to pray over their little brother. It was such a comfort to have people come up to us afterwards, some of whom we had never met before. One after another they shared how much Joseph had touched their lives, and how much they had been praying for him.

That following Monday we took Joseph to the University Hospital to be evaluated. They wanted to check his overall condition, and in particular to expose his blood to various tissue samples. The best news would be that out of 30 or 40 samples, none would show signs of rejection. That first night, I could see that Karen was really tired. Things had gone well. The doctors and residents had been incredibly adept at finding veins in the groin with minimal effort for drawing samples. I sent Karen home and stayed the night with Joseph, feeding every couple of hours. By now, we had been living like a home-based Intensive Care Unit round the clock for nearly four weeks. We were tired, but felt strengthened by this small but realistic hope.

The following morning, Dr. Braunlin came by. I was impressed with her sensitivity and attentiveness. Her main objection to considering the transplant was the length of time that Joseph had been living with his one chamber pumping to both the lungs and to the body. The concern was that the lungs had been experiencing high pressure now for several weeks. A normal heart would pump to the lungs at low pressure. The constricted vessels in the lungs might cause a quick failure. My feeling was that Joseph was doomed to die slowly by starvation if we did not intervene, so Dr. Braunlin agreed to obtain more information from one of the few institutions with experience in infant heart transplants at Loma Linda, California.

All went well till that Thursday. The neurologists desired to do an EEG to have a baseline of Joseph's brain function before surgery, if surgery were performed. Karen was present at the test, calming Joseph down whenever he complained about the airplane glue and wires stuck to his head. Unfortunately, the nurse had been confused about how long it would take. Instead of 20 minutes, it took an hour and a half. Towards the end, Joseph was crying severely, and Karen had to request they stop the test. We had almost lost him once before from stressing himself; we did not wish nearly to lose him again.

The next day, we took Joseph home. He looked worse now, ever since the EEG. We had been given an oxygen tank and a small nasal breathing tube (called a cannula) for him to wear. During the night we came to the realization that administering oxygen while he nursed from his bottle seemed to help tremendously. In retrospect, oxygen might have helped his milk intake during the previous weeks. That morning, Dr. Braunlin came to us and told us that Joseph had passed his tissue rejection tests, and that Loma Linda had indicated that 3 months would be the length of time after which a transplant would not be a viable option.

We took Joseph home. That evening, Dennis talked to us on the phone. The doctors needed reassurance that we were willing to go for it 100% with Joseph. This would mean feeding him by whatever means, IV or through the nose in order to increase his malnourished state. We agreed to these requests and even offered to bring Joseph in that night. Dennis called Dr. Braunlin, who felt it would be O.K. to bring him in the next day.

That last night of having our son home with us was unusual. We slept on the living room floor with him, feeding him every couple of hours, and administering oxygen. In the middle of the night, Karen woke me and asked me to look at him. "What's going on - he looks so good?! " I looked at him and sure enough, he was awake, alert, and happy. Even more incredibly, for the first time since his birth, Joseph' color looked great, a kind of healthy pink. The next morning, he looked grey and bluish once again. But the night was a sign of hope. It was as though the Lord was saying, "Trust Me. I could heal Joseph now if I chose."

That morning there was a simple sign of hope that gave me a sense of peace. While Karen was on the phone, Joseph looked over at his Mom and laughed and smiled. Next, he studied me and did the same thing. Finally, he looked up at the ceiling, which apparently amused him as well. I supposed that Karen and I ranked right up there with the ceiling as far as our son was concerned! Perhaps he saw something we did not see.

We took Joseph to be checked in at the ICU for children. Very soon, they had him hooked up to a gavage food tube through his nose. Actually, he seemed quite comfortable, because now he needed to expend zero effort in order to be fed. The first couple of days he slept a lot, as his tummy got filled every two hours with his Mom's pumped milk. The surgeon came in and suggested that as long as he was stable, we should continue this course of action in order to get Joseph at least back to his birth weight. Otherwise, he may only have a 10% chance of surviving a transplant. This might require one to two weeks. Meanwhile, Dr. Braunlin had planned for some time to take a week of vacation at this time. She obviously felt guilty about leaving us, but since Joseph simply needed to build up his reserves for a week anyway, we were glad she was taking a much-needed break.

That night, we had our first good sleep in over four weeks. The successive days went by smoothly. However, it did seem that Joseph was gradually struggling more with his breathing and required more oxygen as his body tried to assimilate the extra milk. An X-Ray did indicate fluid building in his lungs despite the diuretic.

Then came the MRI. The neurologists felt strongly they wanted to perform an MRI because a CAT scan had shown a slight defect in the brain. The MRI would give the best baseline to indicate whether the defect was changing with time, particularly after the surgery.

The MRI kept getting postponed. Finally, we heard it would probably happen sometime in the late afternoon or early evening. Karen and I went home to feed Lauren and David and then brought them to the hospital. Karen stayed outside in the playground with the kids while I went in to visit Joseph. When I arrived, medical people were surrounding his bed. The head of the ICU was in the process of trying to get a line into our son. Once again, I felt the horror of seeing our beautiful child's life being in jeopardy.

The young resident explained to me that they had given Joseph some mild sedation - benadryl - before going down to the MRI. Once there, they found that he began screaming whenever they put him in the machine. More sedative was used, including chloral hydrate. Again, he was put into the machine, apparently calm but awake. Again he began screaming. This occurred several times until finally Joseph simply began screaming and wouldn't stop. He was angry! The resident gave him maximum sedation to no avail. They gave up and brought him back to the ICU.

Within a few minutes, Joseph began gasping for breath. Monitors indicated that his pulse had dropped from 140 to 70 beats per minutes, and his pressure was way down. Immediately, a team began to get him hooked to the ventilator and endeavored to get IV's into him. This was where Dad walked into the scene.

I went down to the playground. From her vantage point outside, Karen could see the flurry of activity in Joseph's room, and figured something was going on. Needless to say, Karen was overwhelmed with fear and grief. I stayed with

Lauren and David while she called Mike and Christi Mallinger to come and pick them up.

That last night was a long one. We were blessed to have a wonderful male nurse. He saw us praying over Joseph and asked about our church. He shared that he had lost his wife two years ago, leaving him with two small children. Despite the tragedy, his faith hadn't wavered, and he somehow was able to see the loving hand of God in the midst of his sorrow.

During the night, I realized that the heart drugs to make Joseph's heart beat harder were perhaps doing more harm than good. His vitals now were stable in rate, i.e. 140 beats per minute, but his blood pressure was at 30. Once during the night, our nurse turned off the drugs in order to use the line for drawing blood samples. Suddenly, I noticed Joseph's vitals going up a lot. I went to the young resident cardiologist and pleaded with her to stop giving Joseph the drugs for his heart. This, however, contradicted everything the textbooks said about treating a heart failure patient. I'm sure it made no difference to the final outcome, but at the time I was frustrated at the rigidity and lack of common sense I was encountering.

By morning, things looked bad. Joseph had not urinated since the incident began. That implied kidney failure. Blood pressure was still around 30. It had gone up a bit when he received a transfusion, but the effect was temporary. A neurologist came by and looked at various notes and charts. This was bad enough, but when he asked the nurse for a tape measure to measure Joseph's head, Karen had had it! "Do you *really* think his head has grown since yesterday?!" He decided against acquiring this important data and exited the room.

Finally, in the mid-afternoon, Karen started to notice that Joseph's vitals were slowly dropping. The pulse had been 140. Now it was 110 and dropping. She called me in. The nurse likewise contacted the doctor. I kneeled by the bed while Karen stood behind me. Again, I held Joseph's fingers and prayed the Rosary on them while Karen prayed and wept behind me.

"Hail Mary, full of grace..."

At first Karen didn't realize what I was doing. It looked like I was just losing it and babbling incoherently. "What are you doing?!" she asked through her tears.

"Praying the Rosary," I said.

"Oh. OK. Never mind."

"Hail Mary, full of grace..."

Slowly the pulse dropped, 100, 90, 80, ...

"Oh Honey, they're dropping!" Karen cried.

"I know, Hon; he's dying."

"Hail Mary, full of grace..."

I think it was about this time that the dam finally collapsed. Seeing our beautiful baby, gently rolling his tiny fingers like beads as we prayed, waiting next to him helplessly as he began to leave this world, was more than I could hold in.

Tears exploded from my eyes with no effort as minute by minute the pulse continued its downward journey. I would never again be Dad to this little boy in this life. At least, not in the usual human sense. He would never ride a bike, he would never catch a fish, he would never meet and marry a woman who would be the love of his life.

"Hail Mary, full of grace..."

We continued to wait and pray.

After 20 minutes, there was no more pressure reading even though the pulse monitor said 50 beats per minute. The doctor switched off the monitor. "The electrical pulses are deceptive because they can go on for a while even after the heart stops beating."

The doctor attached a manual ventilator so that they could pause the respiration long enough to listen for a heart beat. There was none. "I'm sorry," she said. Within minutes, the nurses disconnected all the tubes and wires so we could hold our son for our last farewell. By now, the room was filled with doctors and nurses from the unit, all of whom were wiping their eyes, and telling us they were sorry.

It was while this was occurring, the actual moment of death, that I experienced an extraordinary conviction or certainty. I had the overwhelming sensation that this beautiful body that lay before me was no longer baby Joseph. One minute before, it was baby Joseph. Now, no longer. Instead it was the body of the baby we had loved and fought to keep alive these last two and a half months. Baby Joseph was still very much real and alive, but his spirit had left the body that had been his until now.

Scientifically I know that "up" and "down" are directions that are determined by gravity. I also am well aware that the clouds and the sky do not constitute Heaven.

But I think that our physical bodies were created, and experience things like gravity and blue sky and clouds, precisely so that in some symbolic tangible way God can communicate a sense or an idea of what Heaven is. So it works for me to "lift up my eyes to the heavens from which my help comes."

In this case, as I watched the last few twitches of my son's body as he left this earth, I had the overwhelming sense of his spirit rising as it left, beginning a new journey, a new form or chapter of life. Looking at a dead person, if death is all there is when death occurs, is a horrible, grim, miserable, and hopeless experience. Looking at a dead person when you feel strongly that this is their body, their body is dead, but the person you love is very much alive and in fact is very free, is of course very sad, very painful, but also very much filled with hope. We have no proof, we cannot easily confirm this hypothesis with a scientific instrument, but our confidence can still be high. We have One who has gone before us.

So there is quiet stillness that occurs after death, a peaceful weariness resulting from the final farewell, the final letting go.

We held our little boy, wrapped in his baby blanket, for several hours. Right away, we called Mike and Christi to bring Lauren and David to come say goodbye to their brother. They touched and held Joseph quite a bit. We talked a lot about the reality of his death. He wasn't asleep, he wasn't breathing, he never would wake up again. We talked about little Joseph being with Jesus now. Lauren soon developed her own theological terminology. The little body was the "dead baby Joseph" while Joseph in Heaven was the "alive baby Joseph". It was about as good a way of expressing it as I could have found.

Special friends soon arrived. Christi was already there, having brought Lauren and David. Soon Randy Mueller appeared, as well as Tom and Laurie Wrobel, and Tom and Cindy Rivard - all from our small group. They simply wept and prayed with us as we thanked our Lord for the unexpected gift of time that we had with Joseph, and for the quality of that time. Our first response was to begin asking our little saint in Heaven to pray for his Mom and Dad to get through this tough time.

There were many blessings along with the grief the following days between Joseph's death and the funeral. We spent a fair amount of time planning the liturgy, the music, the readings etc., and preparing a nice program using the desktop publishing tools I had from 3M. In 1990, printing a program including the use of a photo wasn't as easy as it is today. There was something very healing about honoring our son by trying to allow the celebration to be special. Another blessing was the director of the Kessler funeral home, who stated that he made it a policy not to profit on the funerals of infants. He was true to his word. After expending a good deal of time and effort talking to us, preparing Joseph's body, and performing transportation, he charged virtually nothing for his services. That act of kindness, along with the support of people like Fr. Pat Lannon of Nativity and Theresa Stoelb who was in charge of music for the celebration, really let us feel that God cared for us and had not forsaken us.

So ends Joseph's story on this earth. My son taught me a lifetime of experience about love and pain, and how the two can be closely coupled together. Joseph taught me how to cry my heart out. He tore down my walls of protection that I had taken years to build around myself. Because he taught me how to cry, he also taught me how to pray. He taught me that God does not want a dull, Platonic, cerebral relationship. He wants to know us, and for us to know Him, with our hearts as well as our minds. In so many ways, this little child has been a presence of Christ in our lives.

Our family has been very blessed with a sense of great peace and hope over losing Joseph. Of course there have been times of sadness, times of wishing things could have been different. But the sad memories are also very beautiful, because our memories of Joseph are also very sweet. As our lives slowly returned to "normal" in the ensuing months, I sometimes feared that we would lose the gift of what Joseph taught us.

One thing is for sure. We cannot be bitter or angry at God for what happened. We were privileged to have Joseph, heart and all (although it's not a privilege I would wish upon anyone **else** having a baby!). In their last attempt to save Joseph, the doctors tried to get an IV needle into him anywhere they could. As a result, we noticed after he died that both his hands and feet had many puncture wounds. It seemed fitting, somehow, that upon the hour of his death, our little one should have born the signs of the stigmata. Karen noted that the time was about 3:00 PM, which in Catholic tradition is the hour of Devine Mercy, the hour our

Lord died. As we continue on now in this life, we will need the prayers of all our friends and especially of our little holy one who is in Heaven. My dear little Saint Joseph, pray for us.

Postlude

Almost 25 years have passed since Joseph's departure from our home to his eternal home. Most of what I have written up to this point was written soon after the event. At Joseph's wake, Kathy and the other nurses looked at me sympathetically and asked, "Do you think that you two will consider having children again?" I told them, "I know my wife. Give her a few months and Karen will be ready to become pregnant again." They looked rather stunned and said, "Well, you be ready when she is!" Sure enough, twelve months later Peter Joseph was born. We felt OK about giving Peter his brother's name as his middle name, much like honoring the memory of a deceased parent or grandparent. In no way did we have any thoughts about "replacing" Joseph. Four years later, Michael Anthony, our youngest, was born.

Lauren and David had interesting ways of keeping mindful of the younger brother that they lost. If they got possession of a helium balloon, the two siblings would fight to the death if one tried to steal it from the other. However, after playing with it for a while, either one would let the balloon go, rising up to the heavens, and say, "Here you go, Joseph, have fun with it!"

The most notable event however occurred the Christmas following our loss of Joseph. We had planned to cut down a fresh Christmas tree as was our family tradition. However, it was late in the afternoon and with the darkness soon approaching, we stopped at a green house and chose a tree already cut. Upon returning home, I went to the garage, got the saw, and proceeded to cut 1" off the bottom to ensure a fresh area of wood to draw the water into the rest of the tree. Then, just to be sure, I cut another 1" slice, and proceeded to return the saw to the garage. When I got back to the tree, Karen was there, looking at the tree with awe. "Did you see those chunks of wood?" she asked. I looked, and to my astonishment, the two slices of wood were both in the shape of a perfect heart, with a slight crack in the middle as though it were broken. We looked at the rest of the trunk, and it appeared perfectly round - no indication of the odd heart-shape. I inserted the image of the cracked wooden heart into Joseph's photo for this book – it seemed appropriate.

What better Christmas card for our Lord to send us on Joseph's behalf to let us know he was in good hands, and that he had not forgotten us any more than we had forgotten him! As our memorial to Joseph, we have his photo on the mantle, with the two heart-shaped pieces of wood on either side like bookends.

Our friends Bill and Carolyn Dower purchased a crab apple tree in honor of Joseph. We stood together in the front yard, planted the tree, and Carolyn read a beautiful poem/prayer that she wrote commemorating our son. The tree has grown almost as tall as our 2½ story home almost. While we still live and have memory it will remain "Joseph's Tree".

There's another thing I'd like to mention. This is extremely important if you have gone through a similar experience or know someone who has. We were advised to keep our relationship strong, and to guard against being torn apart by the loss of our child. We later heard that the statistics are extremely poor for marriages after the loss of a child. A recent statistic we read was that 80% end in divorce.

Why is that? Many articles talk about the complexity of rebuilding a marriage and a family after the death of a child. I read a lot of discussion about the uniqueness and isolation of the grieving process for each spouse. Some articles talk about women continuing to grieve for long periods of time, and men suppressing their grief, then moving on with their life by returning to work. I've only known a few women who have lost a child. Perhaps they were unique, but they all seemed to find ways to channel their grief in positive ways.

The articles I read indicated that those who experience deep faith seem to do better than those who do not, unless they try to use their faith as a way of escaping the necessary grieving process. Even people of faith must remember that Christ wept before the tomb of his friend Lazarus.

The marriage statistics we read seem valid based on how surprised our nurses reacted to our handling of the grief process and based on some families that I have known over the years. I'm not a counsellor, and have had no professional training. However, my purely personal observations as a layman are as follows: most women that I have known are much more adept at expressing emotion than most men that I have known. Expressing emotion and sharing feelings makes us vulnerable, and the women I have known seem to find that easier than most guys I have known. I'm sure there are lots of physiological as well as cultural reasons for this.

Combine that with my personal observation that many guys do not have a close friend that they can trust or open up to, and you have a recipe for disaster after a crisis such as we experienced. I was very fortunate during college and during our relocation to Saint Paul, MN from out east, to be welcomed into groups of men and women who were committed to forming deeper bonds than "How is it going?" "OK." Not all churches or faith communities will necessarily have a sense of true personal sharing, but I was fortunate to have found such groups both times.

Although I was still a bottled-up person in many ways (due to upbringing and temperament), sharing was something I had learned to do by this time, and so sharing came naturally. I could tell that the joint sharing that Karen and I did with the nurses as we went through our Joseph adventure was somewhat atypical, which explained their surprise.

By contrast, I have personally witnessed situations where families have lost a child, and their marriages did not go well for many years. The phenomenon I observed was that whereas the mother of the child grieved and wept and shared everything she was feeling with friends and family, the stoic father held it together and was silent and strong. This worked during the busy time of making decisions and preparing for funerals, but did not work so well in the subsequent months ahead. Gradually, the pain of loss, which is I can tell you nearly unbearable at times, would eat away at the father's heart, and some form of solace and comfort had to be found.

So whether it was an extra-marital affair, alcohol or drug abuse, or unexplained anger issues that never had been a problem before, the grief does express itself. If the grief isn't processed in a healthy way, it comes out sideways in some form of negative behavior that may be so severe that it can lead to divorce.

So to all guys (or gals) who like myself don't find it easy to make close friends or to share in a real way with others, my suggestion is that whatever your faith tradition or highest calling is, find a community of people or a circle of friends who are willing to share, and whom you can trust with your deepest emotions.

I can say unequivocally that our marriage was made much deeper and stronger by enduring this terrible thing together. If handled correctly, something tragic like the loss of a child can have the same sad beauty as a sad but wonderful book or a movie. Sharing that story together, remembering it together, becomes yet another unique bond that only the two of you will share, and makes your spouse *more* indispensable, not less, to your existence.

I don't think it registered how deep an impact Joseph had on our family until some time went by. I remember one afternoon Lauren was playing with a toy in the living room when suddenly she threw herself on the floor crying uncontrollably: "I miss Joseph so much – it's not fair - he was my best friend!" After weeping for several minutes, she sat right back up, as though to say "Glad to get that out of my system," and proceeded to continue where she left off playing with her toy.

When David was several years older, one night he came

into our room late at night. "I had a terrible dream. Lauren was choking on something, and couldn't get it out. She was suffocating. I don't want my sister to die!" This was rather out of character for a typical younger brother who generally felt tormenting his sister was his primary job description.

For me personally, however, the impact was quite dramatic. As I mentioned earlier, I strongly take after my British physicist father. Neither Brits nor physicists are renowned for their expressive emotion. Combine the above with natural shyness and bookishness, and you have one fairly repressed person. Thanks to a profound conversion in high school and college, I had come a long way to being able to express love and affection. Expressing anger or grief however still eluded me. I feared the uncontrolled outpouring of either emotion.

It was a year after Joseph's death. Karen and I went to see *Les Miserables* at the Orpheum theater with our friends Tom and Laurie. I had a rough idea of the plot of the book and of the musical. I was not prepared for the death scene of Fantine. The pent up year of sadness, grief, and sorrow over losing our little boy exploded like a hot steam kettle of tears. I understood what Victor Hugo was expressing through Fantine. I understood how love, sorrow, hope, and death can mingle together to create a fabric of unbearable pain, tearing the heart into pulsating shreds of longing for that which can never be.

Likewise, the death scene of Jean Val-Jean at the end, where Fantine appears to welcome him to heaven, was more than I could bear. The beauty and the hope of seeing our little boy, perhaps as a young man in his prime some day, made we weep with joy at the possibility that I, too, might have the privilege of a good death. When all is said and done, and all the prizes and promotions have been achieved, what really matters more at the moment of our death than the legacy of love we have left behind and the promise of new life and continuing love that we have been given for the future?

As our journey through life continues, and we move closer to our eventual departure from this world, we feel a close link to that ultimate destination that no one here on earth has ever seen. We know that Joseph is waiting there patiently for us, that our Lord is keeping him quite busy with prayers of intercession for his remaining family. So again, we pray now as we did 25 years ago, our little Saint Joseph, pray for us!

www.ingramcontent.com/pod-product-compliance
Lightning Source LLC
Chambersburg PA
CBHW071024040426
42443CB00007B/920

9 780099 633792